PIANO
VOCAL
GUITAR

Kirk Frank... SONGS

VOLUME 1

ISBN-13: 978-1-4234-2570-0
ISBN-10: 1-4234-2570-7

HAL•LEONARD®
CORPORATION
7777 W. BLUEMOUND RD. P.O. BOX 13819 MILWAUKEE, WI 53213

Visit Hal Leonard Online at
www.halleonard.com

HE WILL TAKE THE PAIN AWAY

Words and Music by
KIRK FRANKLIN

LET ME TOUCH YOU

Words and Music by
KIRK FRANKLIN

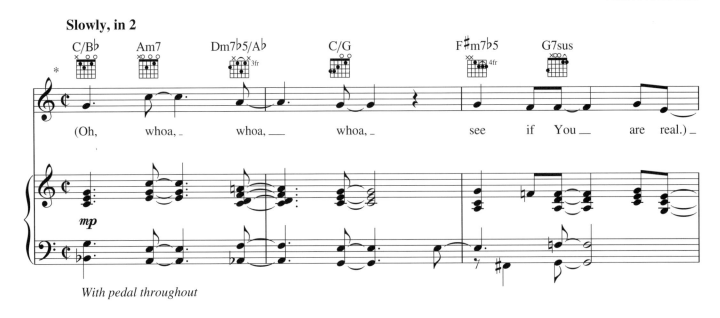

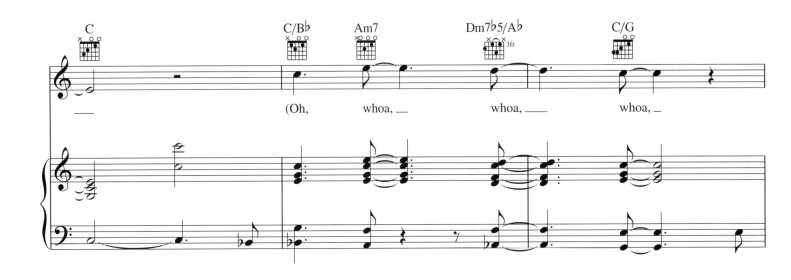

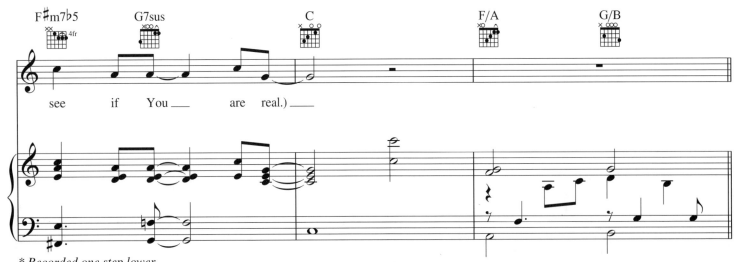

* *Recorded one step lower.*

WHEN I GET THERE

Words and Music by
KIRK FRANKLIN

CONQUERORS

Words and Music by
KIRK FRANKLIN

Moderately, in 2

With pedal throughout

mor - row is _____
seen His face, _____

a

WHEN YOU FALL

Words and Music by
KIRK FRANKLIN

BLESSING IN THE STORM

Words and Music by
KIRK FRANKLIN

* *Recorded a half step higher.*

THE STORM IS OVER NOW

Words and Music by
KIRK FRANKLIN

YOU ARE

Words and Music by
KIRK FRANKLIN

Slowly, in 2

With pedal throughout

Je - sus, You
Je - sus, You

are my Joy with - in. You are the Shel -
are my Cor - ner - stone. You are my Friend

* Recorded a step lower.

A/C♯
Bm9
- ter from the wind. You're the For - giv -
when I'm a - lone. You're the Con - vic -
Em11
5fr
A13sus
- er of my sins,
- tor when I'm wrong,
A7
A/G
D/F♯
D9
4fr
Je - sus, You are, yes. Where can I go?
Je - sus, You are, yes. You are the Peace
Gmaj7
E/G♯
1
A
Who can I call? Who's there to catch
with - in my soul.

THE FAMILY WORSHIP MEDLEY

Words and Music by
KIRK FRANKLIN

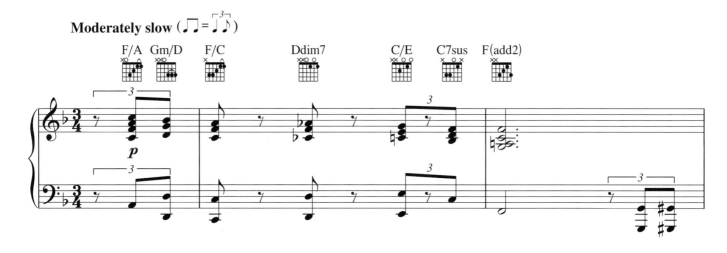

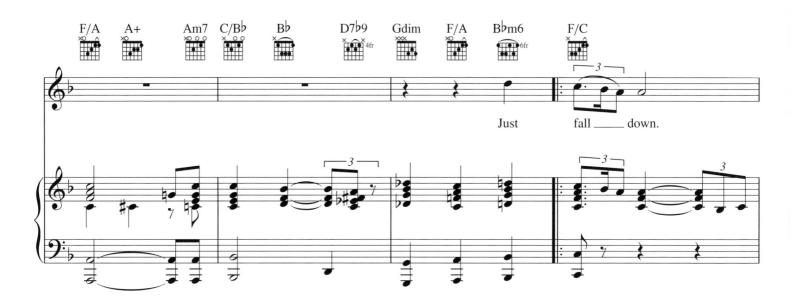

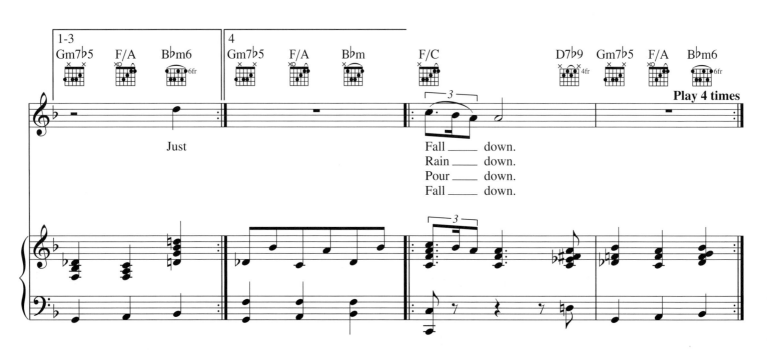

MELODIES FROM HEAVEN

Words and Music by
KIRK FRANKLIN

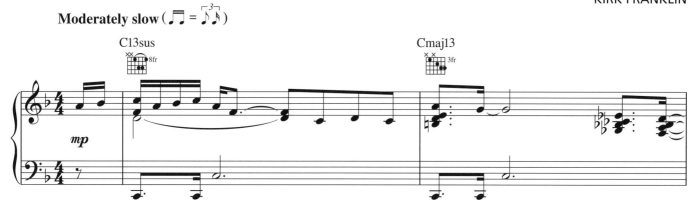

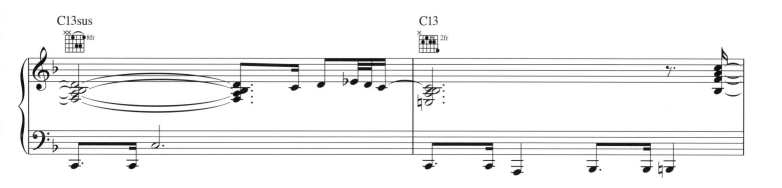

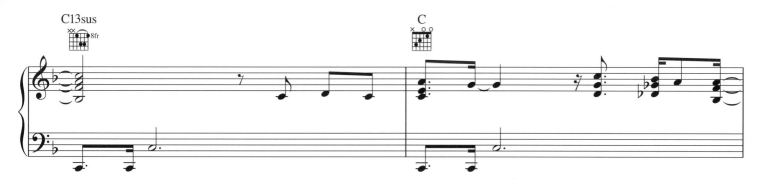

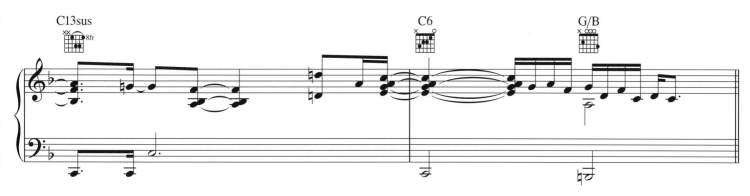

LOOK AT ME NOW

Words and Music by
KIRK FRANKLIN

Per-se-cut-ed, crit-i-cized,___ been de-nied___ and a-ban-

doned. Pushed a-way, giv-en a-way,___ some days I could-n't i-mag-

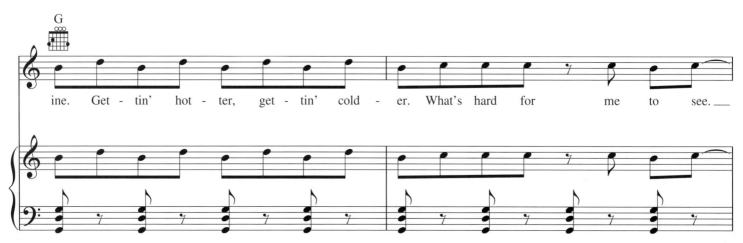

ine. Get-tin' hot-ter, get-tin' cold-er. What's hard for me to see.___

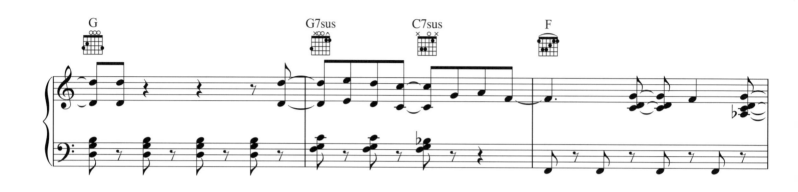

(Spoken:) I want everybody just to realize...   *that God is doing a work in your life right now.*

(Look at ___ me.)

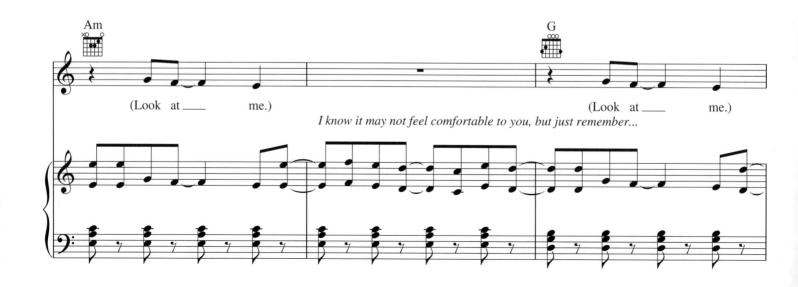

(Look at ___ me.)   (Look at ___ me.)

I know it may not feel comfortable to you, but just remember...